Winner

2002 Gwen Pharis Ringwood Award for Drama of the
Alberta Literary Awards
2001 Dr. Betty Mitchell Award for Best New Play
2000 Alberta National Playwriting Competition

"Massicotte doesn't push his anti-war message. He doesn't have to. The charm of his romance juxtaposed against prosaic descriptions from the trenches... do it for him." —*San Francisco Chronicle*

"Massicotte writes with an earnestness that is rare in this cynical day and age. His gift for pulling at the heart strings cannot be denied." —*San Jose Mercury News*

"A play that understands loving and grieving and shakes you with the horrible immediacy of war." —*Orlando Sentinel*

"Massicotte is a gifted storyteller with an ear for detail and imagery. There was nary a dry eye in the house by the time the actors took their final bows." —*Edmonton Journal*

"*Mary's Wedding* is an unabashed tear-jerker that is sentimental in the way that stories of doomed love are, but this sentiment is almost impossible to resist." —*Oakland Tribune*

"This marvellous new Canadian play is certain to make immediate and lasting connections with anyone who has experienced loss... and had to move on." —*Regina Leader Post*

"*Mary's Wedding* is a treat. Based on true historical battles, it does so much more than bring war close for examination. It brings love that much closer." —*Victoria Weekend Edition*

"*Mary's Wedding* sets about doing, and on a bare stage, what a novel can easily do on a page: to move fluidly through the landscape of mind and memory." —*Edmonton Journal*

"Massicotte blends a war story that could well be a two-act action play, and the story of two lovers intriguing enough to be a two-act conventional romance, into a one-act tightly constructed play, but never seems to be slighting either story." —*Potomac Stages*, Washington DC

"The opening-night audience sat entranced and the final moments are some of the most heart-wrenching I have experienced in a theatre in a long time." —*Edmonton Sun*

"*Mary's Wedding* is ultimately a genuine, simple love story with innocent intentions to invoke pure emotional response."
—*Metro Weekly*, Washington DC

"*Mary's Wedding* has audiences breathing in at the first words and only consciously exhaling after the last scene ends." —*Victoria Rainbow News*

"Massicotte's play about love, separation and regret is an unpretentious winner... lyrical, warm and sweet spirited, a love story that avoids mushiness, a war story that doesn't assault us with earnest speeches."
—*Ottawa Citizen*

"Massicotte's play is simple, too—deceptively so, in that its uncomplicated story contains a world of experience."
—*Washington City Paper*

"Among other things, Massicotte has done his history homework and manages to convey an amazing amount of information in an engrossing, personal way. If you didn't remember that bayonets and aeroplanes co-existed in one war, here's your chance to see how in action."
—*New York Theatre Wire*

"The ending really is quite extraordinary in it's emotional impact."
—CBC Radio Canada

"Covering first love thwarted by war, how loving someone strongly is as frightening as it is exhilarating, and companionship in war, the play's dream setting now in this revival achieves full effect." —*Edinburgh Guide*

Mary's Wedding

Mary's Wedding
Stephen Massicotte

Playwrights Canada Press
Toronto • Ontario

PLAYWRIGHTS CANADA PRESS
The Canadian Drama Publisher
215 Spadina Ave., Suite 230, Toronto, Ontario Canada M5T 2C7
phone 416.703.0013   fax 416.408.3402
orders@playwrightscanada.com • www.playwrightscanada.com

For professional or amateur production rights, please contact
Chris Till, Creative Artists Agency
162 5th Avenue, 6th Floor
New York, NY 10010
(212) 277-9000

The publisher acknowledges the support of the Canadian taxpayers through the Government of Canada Book Publishing Industry Development Program, the Canada Council for the Arts, the Ontario Arts Council, and the Ontario Media Development Corporation.

Cover photo of bride by Nancy R. Cohen
Cover design by Stephen Massicotte
Type design by Blake Sproule

LIBRARY AND ARCHIVES CANADA CATALOGUING IN PUBLICATION

Massicotte, Stephen
Mary's wedding / Stephen Massicotte. -- 2nd ed.

A play.
ISBN 978-0-88754-899-4

I. Title.

PS8576.A79668M37 2009   C812'.6   C2009-904749-7

First edition: June 2002
Second edition: September 2009
Printed and bound in Canada by Gauvin Press, Gatineau

for Robin

Letter from Lt. Gordon Muriel Flowerdew
to his mother. Letter courtesy of LdSH
(RC), Regimental Museum and Archives.

Lieutenant Gordon Muriel Flowerdew was awarded the Victoria Cross for leading C Squadron, the Lord Strathcona's Horse Regiment, in the charge at Moreuil Wood on the thirtieth of March, 1918. He died of his wounds on the thirty-first of March, at No. 41 Casualty Clearing Station. This letter was postmarked in the field with the same date, and arrived in England on the fourth of April, 1918.

Lt. Gordon Muriel Flowerdew. Above photo and letter (opposite page) courtesy of LdSH (RC), Reginmental Museum and Archives.

"Dearest Mother,

Have been a bit busy lately, so haven't been able to write. I managed to borrow this card. Haven't had any mail for some days, so we are very keen to see the papers. The weather is still very good, but very keen at night. Have had the most wonderful experiences lately and wouldn't have missed it for the anything— Best love to all.

    Your affectionate son,

    Gordon"

He is buried at Namps-au-Val British Cemetery, France, eleven miles southwest of Amiens. Plot I. Row H. Grave I. The first day of rehearsal for the first production of this play took place on January 2, 2002. This was the 117th anniversary of his birthday.

        —SM

Mary's Wedding was first produced at playRites '02, Alberta Theatre Projects's annual festival of new Canadian plays, in Calgary, February, 2002, with the following cast and crew:

CHARLIE   Collin Doyle
MARY/FLOWERS   Sarah M. Smith

Directed by Gina Wilkinson
Set Designed by Scott Reid
Costumes Designed by David Boechler
Lighting Designed by Melinda Sutton
Composer/Sound Designer: Bob Doble
Festival Dramaturge: Vanessa Porteous
Assistant Dramaturge: Vicki Stroich
Production Stage Manager: Dianne Goodman
Stage Manager: Crystal Beatty
Assistant Stage Manager: Karen Fleury
University of Calgary Intern: Angela Bewick

Characters
Charlie
Mary
Flowers

For a while, in the deep blue and green darkness, the sound of a light breeze can be heard. The young actor playing the role of CHARLIE emerges from the shadows.

CHARLIE   Hello, out there. Thank you for coming. Before we begin there is something I have to tell you.

Tonight is the night before Mary's wedding. It's a July wedding on a Saturday morning in nineteen hundred and twenty, two years after the end of the Great War, or as you might know it now, the First World War.

So, tomorrow is Mary's wedding, tonight is just a dream. I ask you to remember that. It begins at the end and ends at the beginning. There are sad parts.

Don't let that stop you from dreaming it too.

Mary's Wedding

A barefoot girl in a nightgown enters.

MARY It always starts the same. I dream it is dawn, in a field. I'm in my wedding dress. I'm out there looking for flowers for my bouquet. It is a quiet and peaceful morning.

Then I see someone walking through the grass. At first he is no one in particular, just a figure walking, but then I see that I know him. He has a face I know well.

He smiles and I follow his eyes to a horse sleeping in the damp grass. She wakes from her dream and stands up. He steps by her neck and shoulder and touches and calms her. It has been a long, cold night but the morning sun warms them.

That's when it starts to rain, slowly at first, then heavier and heavier. He and his horse don't move and I always wonder why. It's raining very hard and they should find some shelter, a tree, or a barn... somewhere, but they don't. He just stands there, looking up into the rainstorm, getting ready to count the thousands from the flash to the rumble.

I call to them. They never hear me but I call to them anyway. RUN, CHARLIE, RUN! PLEASE! Ride away from there. Get in from the storm. But they can't hear me. They never hear me. They just stand very still.

Then, just before a white flash like lightning cuts them into sharp outline, he says something I cannot make out.

CHARLIE ...

MARY   Then it goes dark.

                A flash and darkness.

                And before the words Charlie says form into under-
                standing in my head... there is thunder.

                Thunder. Rain falls outside an old barn.

                When I can see again, I am running down the turn in
                the road, down from the bridge into the old barn. This
                is years ago. It's a downpour and I've been caught in it.
                I'm soaking wet. I'm late. My mother will be worried.

                Inside, it smells of wood, old rope, and... horse.

                *CHARLIE and his horse are in the barn staring upward, as
                they were in the field. Outside, a thunderstorm approaches with
                a far-off flash of lightning.*

CHARLIE   One-one thousand, two-one thousand, three-one thou-
                sand, four-one thousand, five-one thousand...

                Thunder rumbles.

MARY   Was that just five?

CHARLIE   Shhh!

                Pause.

MARY   Is it coming closer?

CHARLIE   What does it sound like?

MARY   You're more frightened than your horse is.

CHARLIE   What makes you think I'm afraid?

Lightning flashes closer. CHARLIE flinches.

MARY　　　　Oh, nothing at all...

CHARLIE　　One-one thousand, two-one thousand, three-one thousand, four-one thous...

Thunder.

CHARLIE　　Shit! /　　MARY　　That was closer!

MARY laughs.

MARY　　　　Oh.

CHARLIE　　I'm sorry, I swear too much. I'm trying to quit. It's coming closer.

MARY　　　　I hope so. I love thunderstorms.

CHARLIE　　I'm not afraid... I just don't like getting caught out in the rain so much.

MARY　　　　Only the rain? You're not a bit frightened of the thunder and lightning?

CHARLIE　　No... well, a little bit. When I was six a tree in the schoolyard got hit by lightning. It sounded like a whip crack right beside your ear. We all jumped out of our seats. Mister MacKenzie, our teacher, had been reading "The Charge of the Light Brigade" to us. When he jumped he threw the book.

MARY　　　　He didn't.

CHARLIE　　A kid in the third desk got hit in the back of the head...

MARY　　　　Really?

CHARLIE   Yes, sir, with Tennyson.

               MARY smiles.

               Flash! Bang! It hit the tree out in the yard. Split the
               branch with the swing. Scorched it right off.

               MARY looks doubtful.

               The branch was this big around.

               MARY laughs.

               Well, what if you were in that swing? If that lightning
               had hit you? You wouldn't laugh then. Ha, ha.

MARY   Of course not, but you weren't hit, were you? The chan-
               ces of you being in that swing in that rainstorm at that
               exact moment are very small. Almost impossible...

               Lightning flashes.

CHARLIE   One-one thousand, two-one thousand, thr...

               Thunder.

               Shh... shh... easy there. Easy. See? Horses know.

MARY   It's coming closer, then it'll pass. There's nothing to be
               frightened about.

CHARLIE   Yes, there is.

MARY   Only if you mind getting a little wet.

               A close bolt of lightning flashes.

CHARLIE   One-one thou...

*Thunder claps almost simultaneous with the lightning.
CHARLIE is visibly shaken.*

MARY   Shh, shh, it's going to be all right. Just a bit more and it
              will be over. Shh, shh, do you know what? Whenever I'm
              afraid, I just talk to myself.

CHARLIE   Talk to yourself?

MARY   Sometimes I sing a song, or I recite a poem, a part of
              something I can remember, and everything turns out
              fine. Do you know any poems?

CHARLIE   "The Charge of the Light Brigade"?

MARY   How does it go?

CHARLIE   I don't remember all of it.

                      Lightning flashes.

MARY   I'll help you. / **CHARLIE**   One-one thousand...

                      Thunder.

MARY   "Half a league..."

CHARLIE   "Half a league, half a league forward..."

MARY   Onward.

CHARLIE   Onward, right... "All in the valley of Death,
              Rode the six hundred.
              'Onward the Light Brigade...'"

MARY   Forward.

CHARLIE   "'Forward the Light Brigade!'
              'Charge for the guns!' he said

Into the valley of Death
Rode the six hundred."

Lightning flashes.

MARY   "'Forward, the Light Brigade!'
Was there a man dismay'd?"

Thunder.

BOTH   "Not tho' the soldier knew
Someone had blunder'd.
Theirs not to make reply,
Theirs not to reason why,
Theirs but to do or die.
Into the valley of Death
Rode the six hundred."

A flicker of lightning.

One-one thousand, two-one thousand, three-one thousand, four-one thousand, five...

A fading roll of thunder sounds.

MARY   See?

CHARLIE   It's going away.

MARY   They always do. Well.

BOTH   What's your name?

Sorry.

MARY   Mary Chalmers.

CHARLIE   I'm Charles Edwards. Charlie, really.

MARY   Nice to meet you, Charlie Edwards.

CHARLIE   I don't know you. I mean, I've lived here all my life and I know most everybody, I don't think I've ever seen... met you before.

MARY   My mother and I just arrived here to join my father.

CHARLIE   Where from?

MARY   From England. "To live with the colonists in the wilds of the Canadas"; as my mother put it. We crossed the Atlantic on a liner.

CHARLIE   I've never seen the ocean. What was it like?

MARY   Blue.

CHARLIE   I thought that it might be... blue.

MARY   I still dream of it sometimes.

CHARLIE   You dream a lot?

MARY   Oh, all the time, the most lovely dreams.

CHARLIE   Me too.

MARY   What are yours about?

CHARLIE   Oh, I don't know. Barns. Not quite as exciting as crossing the ocean.

MARY   Oh, I think barns are very exciting. They're all the rage in London.

The last sounds of the rain have faded.

The storm has gone. Mmm, I love the smell after a rain.

Stephen Massicotte

CHARLIE   That, I do like.

MARY   Well then, I guess we can go.

CHARLIE   There's no sense hiding out in here all night.

MARY   Yes. Oh, I'm so late. My mother will think I was abducted by savages.

CHARLIE   I could give you a ride home. We'll have you there in no time.

MARY   It's not that far.

CHARLIE   There's plenty of room for the both of us.

MARY   I shouldn't really.

CHARLIE   Are you afraid of something?

MARY   He swings the barn door open and the sky is sunset blue clear with one bright star and more coming. The smell of trees and grass after a rain pushes the stuffy barn away.

    Charlie seems to change. He reaches with his arms and puts his foot into the stirrup and pulls himself up. He is now ten feet tall above me.

CHARLIE   Are you coming up? Take my hand.

    MARY takes CHARLIE's hand. The stars bloom as they fill up the sky.

MARY   I'm up in the saddle. I can't do anything but move closer to him.

CHARLIE   Hold on, Mary. You'll be home soon.

MARY   The long blades of grass blend together and blur. The
             fence posts smudge as they rise up and by. One, two,
             three four five-six. A bird flashes across our path. His
             wings flicker three times and he pushes himself, flicker
             three times and we're gone by him.

             The evening air has turned to wind as our horse's hooves
             drum out and splash through puddles in the road.
             Charlie's horse breathes as she runs. In out, in out, shh
             ha, shh ha, shh ha. Our hooves thunder and pound and
             splash, thunder and splash right onto the hollow wood
             of the bridge. The bridge goes by with a deep brown
             rumble. Then splash on the other side. Shh ha, shh ha,
             shh ha.

             I think it is fear that I am feeling. At least, I think it's
             fear; the speed, the noise. Breathing and thundering,
             with this boy that was terrified and hiding one moment
             and fearless and flying with me the next. Fearless and
             flying with me, body to body beside him.

             And when I finally know that what I'm feeling is not
             fear but something new... when I finally have an idea
             that what I am feeling is something entirely differ-
             ent... Charlie is already gone. And I am walking up the
             thirty stones to my mother's front door. I am walking
             the thirty wet stones and my heart is still breathing and
             thundering as fast as a charge. And my feet, my feet are
             carrying me as slowly as a snail.

             That night, I dream only of Charlie. I hear church bells.
             I dream of white dresses, flowers, and little babies and
             Charlie is there for all of it. I see him with horses. I see
             him running with them, riding, in fields, in forests, in

evenings and in mornings. I see him riding and smiling down to the sea.

I see him on an ocean liner. I am watching him sail away. The war is on and the Canadians are sailing for England, then France, and before long the heart of Germany.

CHARLIE   I can't believe it. We are finally joining the fight. Me, Trooper Edwards, First Troop, C Squadron, the Lord Strathcona's Horse Regiment.

They wave goodbye on the wharf.

MARY   The strange thing is, I was never here. I was at home, in my room.

I was never here with the people on the shore. This is not how we said goodbye. When Charlie sailed, I was two days away by train.

Crowds cheer and a marching band plays.

Oh, but it's like a great big birthday party. The sun is shining. The St. Lawrence is glittering. There are children waving and babies in mother's arms. All those arms and voices.

The sound of the ocean rises and a ship's horn sounds.

CHARLIE   Thirty thousand men, seven thousand horses on thirty-eight ocean liners. What'll they do when they see us coming?

MARY   The bands and pipes play across the waves and the men on the decks all wave back.

CHARLIE   Look at that! Isn't that something?

MARY   I'll see you, Charlie!

CHARLIE   I'll charge the Germans for you. Remember me and before long, I'll be home.

BOTH   Hooray, hooray, hooray!

CHARLIE   I'll see you, Mary! I'll be home soon!

BOTH   I'm going to marry that boy. / I'm going to marry that girl.

CHARLIE   Dear Mary...

The weather has been good every day out of the St. Lawrence. Someone "volunteered" First Troop to make the crossing on the ship with the horses. Every inch of the boat is filled with them so they've got us sleeping up on deck in hammocks.

MARY   The ships move like ghosts, steadily humming through the Atlantic. They're not pretty white like I remember them from when I was a girl. They've been painted grey to make them harder to spot by enemy U-boats. Not a ship has a light on. No bands are playing in golden ball-rooms. There is only the steady hum of the ships and the breathing of men in hammocks and horses warming the walls with their bodies.

There are thousands of stars, the moon, and the single coal of a cigarette farther along the deck. It glows and dims on a face before flicking and falling to the silver waves. Nice night.

CHARLIE   Yes, it is that. You on watch?

MARY   Just out for a walk.

CHARLIE   Is that you?

MARY   Of course it's me.

CHARLIE   Sergeant Flowerdew?

MARY   And in the dream I am that sergeant.

CHARLIE stands to attention.

CHARLIE   I'm sorry, sir, I thought you were someone else.

FLOWERS   Who'd you think I was? A girl in a nightie? As you were, man, and don't call me sir, I work for a living.

CHARLIE relaxes.

You on watch?

CHARLIE   I was earlier. Now, I just can't sleep.

FLOWERS   What's the problem?

CHARLIE   Just thinking.

FLOWERS   What about?

CHARLIE   A girl, Sergeant.

FLOWERS   Well, if you've got to be up all night thinking, that's the best thing to be thinking about. Your first crossing, Edwards?

CHARLIE   Yes, Sergeant. This is the first time I've seen the ocean. I've heard good things about it though.

FLOWERS   It's very calm, bright.

CHARLIE   Blue.

FLOWERS   It was like this when I crossed over to Canada.

CHARLIE	Where from?
FLOWERS	From England.
CHARLIE	You can see for miles. You'd think if they were out there... if the U-boats were out there, they could see us pretty good... if they were near here looking for us... they'd have some easy shooting.
FLOWERS	That's why we don't smoke on deck.
CHARLIE	...
FLOWERS	What's her name? Your girl's name?
CHARLIE	Mary, Sergeant.
FLOWERS	Mary Sergeant?
CHARLIE	No, Mary Chalmers. I don't know any Mary Sergeant.
FLOWERS	Charlie and Mary.
CHARLIE	Mary and Charlie. It doesn't really ring, does it?
FLOWERS	It rings just fine. Try going through your life with a name like Flowerdew, Gordon Muriel Flowerdew. They used to call me Flowers when I was a boy... I just told you, so I imagine it'll be all over the regiment before we see land.
CHARLIE	I won't tell the regiment your nickname if you don't tell them I was afraid and couldn't sleep.
FLOWERS	Listen, Charlie, we're horse soldiers, this sailing isn't our kind of war. We'll be on land soon enough, back on our horses, where we belong. Then if we get to France and the Germans before the war is over, they'll be in for it. Eh?

CHARLIE   Maybe we'll take them in a charge, then they'll be in for
                 it.

FLOWERS   Can I give you some advice? From someone with some
                 experience dreaming of someone far away?

                      CHARLIE nods.

                 Don't think about her too much. Or you won't be able
                 to see anything else—you'll see her in everyone, every-
                 where you look.

CHARLIE   I already do.

FLOWERS   Get some sleep. We've got a big day ahead of us tomor-
                 row, feeding horses and shovelling sh… there's a lot of
                 shovelling, let me tell you.

CHARLIE   Yes, Sergeant.

                      CHARLIE takes up the loading of bags.

FLOWERS   There's a lot of bags to be carried as well.

CHARLIE   Yes, Sergeant.

FLOWERS   Rest those shoulders.

CHARLIE   I'll try.

                      *The ship fades over to the town at noon. CHARLIE loads the
                      wagon and whistles "Rule Brittania."*

MARY   How is the work coming along?

CHARLIE   Fine. Oh, good morning.

MARY   Good morning to you. I wasn't sure you recognized me.

CHARLIE   Oh, I did. I do. I mean, I did, how are you?

MARY   I'm, well… I'm me.

CHARLIE   I thought you were you… but I wasn't sure you'd recognize me.

MARY   Oh, I did… it just took a moment.

CHARLIE   Well, I'm dry and there's no storm, and I'm not shaking.

MARY   That's why. Charles "Charlie" Edwards. I remember.

            This a few days after we first met in the barn. This really happened. Well, most of it. He was in town, loading his father's wagon. I always see him first. I wonder if he'll recognize me. Then he sees me too. We play a little game. It's called "we don't see each other at all… oh, hello!"

CHARLIE   Oh, hello!

MARY   Oh, hello! I'm in town… picking up the post.

CHARLIE   Looks like you've got it.

MARY   My mother is organizing the church tea this Saturday.

CHARLIE   Oh. Tea. Saturday?

MARY   You haven't heard? It is becoming quite the event. My mother loves to make a good impression.

CHARLIE   I don't go to very many teas.

MARY   I don't like them much either.

CHARLIE   Oh, I don't know if I like them or not. I'd have to go to know for sure. Are you going to be there?

MARY   Yes. I'll be there.

CHARLIE   Well, good.

MARY   Well, I guess, I should be getting along.

CHARLIE   Um... the other day... during the storm, thank you for
                helping me to remember the poem. Maybe someday I'll
                be able to return the favour.

MARY   Oh, no trouble. Thank you, for the ride home. It was...
                it was, um... nice.

CHARLIE   It was nice, wasn't it? And sorry about the swearing.

MARY   Not at all. I swear all the time. Bloody hell, damn, damn,
                bloody hell, bullocks! Rest those shoulders.

                That's how it happened in town. That's what we said.
                More or less. But we were happier to see each other than
                we both let on. We were playing a game. It's called "try
                not to let your heart fly out of your mouth."

                MARY looks through her mail as she walks. Behind her,
                CHARLIE picks up a letter.

CHARLIE   Ah, Mary! You dropped something.

MARY   Wouldn't my mother be ecstatic? Thank you. Charlie?

CHARLIE   What is it?

MARY   It's from you.

CHARLIE   Really?

MARY   It's from England.

CHARLIE   From England?

MARY   When you go off to the war.

CHARLIE   Do I write you a lot when I'm away?

MARY   "Trooper Charlie Edwards."

CHARLIE   Well? Are you going to open it?

MARY   Can I?

CHARLIE   Open it. Open it.

                         She opens the letter.

MARY   "Dear Mary." Look, that's me.

CHARLIE   Dear Mary.

MARY   "Well, you'll be glad to hear we've made the crossing without being sunk by U-boats."

CHARLIE   That's a relief.

MARY   "I've never been to the city, but our camp in England seems like one. I've never seen so many people in one place at one time. And everyone, to the man, is eager to get over to the front and give it to the Germans. I've seen some sights since I left home but the biggest thrill yet has been a meeting with King George."

CHARLIE   That's right, Mary, I met the King of England...

MARY   You fibber.

CHARLIE   Me and the rest of the division.

MARY   "There we were, more than twenty thousand of us, from British Columbia to Nova Scotia—infantry, cavalry, artillery, all Canadians, all formed up and ready. We practised for a week in the rain for his inspection. They tell us not to look around on parade but I couldn't help looking at him as he rode past."

CHARLIE   He was much smaller than I thought he would be but his beard was exactly like in the painting in the school-house. You're not going to believe this but just as he rode by... the sun came out and he looked right at me.

MARY   He didn't.

CHARLIE   He did too. Right at me.

MARY   Then what happened?

CHARLIE   Well, Flowers caught me staring...

MARY   "Edwards, shut your trap, you're not catching flies."

CHARLIE   I don't think the king heard though.

MARY   "His visit meant that some of us would get our chance to go to the front and it wasn't long before the infantry went over."

CHARLIE   They looked a proud bunch as they marched out to cross the channel. We formed up on parade and cheered them as they left.

MARY   "They went into the line at a place called...?"

CHARLIE   Wipers, we call it.

MARY   Oh, Ypres.

CHARLIE   Yp-res.

MARY   "They had a tough go of it over there, as you may have read in the papers."

CHARLIE   Chlorine gas.

MARY   I did read it in the papers. No one ever used poison gas before. In the front trench, our men looked over as green clouds of fog rose up from the German lines and drifted along with the wind. It crept through the shell craters of no man's land, filling the hollows in the land, but always teased by the wind, towards our lines. We heard it made you feel like you're drowning.

CHARLIE   But our boys were the only ones that held on, see?

            CHARLIE takes the letter and reads on.

            "They put up a tough fight and we're all proud of them."

MARY   The front trenches were filled like a mass grave. We read that in one day six thousand men were lost. Captured, wounded, dead. All those arms and voices.

CHARLIE   "They came to the cavalry and asked us to volunteer to go into the trenches dismounted—as infantry—to make up for the losses..."

MARY   They asked you to give up your horses?

CHARLIE   It's not something any good cavalry man wants to do but... the king looked right at me.

MARY   You said yes, didn't you?

CHARLIE   Every one of us. To the man.

MARY   I'm proud of you. Thank you for writing. I love your letters.

CHARLIE   There'll be more.

MARY   Promise.

CHARLIE   Promise to write you all the time.

MARY   I'll be waiting. I should get home to help Mother with
               the preparations.

CHARLIE   I've got to get this home.

MARY   I'll see you then?

CHARLIE   Maybe at the tea.

MARY   Maybe at the tea. If it's not raining.

CHARLIE   Maybe even then.

                      The Saturday-afternoon tea.

MARY   And I'm at the tea, helping to make sure everything hap-
               pens according to my mother's carefully orchestrated
               plans. Ladies and gentlemen talk in circles, according
               to plan. The pies are brought out, right on schedule,
               according to plan. I look all over the place for Charlie.
               And there he is. Oh, he looks like a proper gentleman.
               He even combed his hair.

CHARLIE   Good afternoon, Miss Chalmers.

MARY   Charles, good afternoon, sir. I didn't expect to see you
               here.

CHARLIE   But it's such a lovely day for a tea.

MARY   Well, don't leave us in suspense, what do you make of it?

CHARLIE   I've never really been to a tea, I mean I've had tea, but not
               been to a tea, so I couldn't really know for sure, until I'd
               actually been to a tea.

MARY   Well, now that you've actually been to one, how do you like it?

CHARLIE   It's nice, it's a tea, there's tea.

MARY   There is tea.

CHARLIE   To tell you the truth, I don't quite feel like I belong.

MARY   Then you are doing very well because you certainly look like you belong.

CHARLIE   Really?

MARY   Yes, you look like a regular tea-goer. A veteran of many teas.

CHARLIE   Charge!

MARY   Your hair looks nice.

CHARLIE   I... I comb it every day. I just combed it more today. I couldn't quite get all of it to stay down.

MARY   There is a bit standing up.

CHARLIE   Where?

MARY   Just a bit. At the back.

                     CHARLIE pats at his hair.

CHARLIE   Did I get it?

MARY   Still... it's...

CHARLIE   How's that?

MARY   Here, hold this, let me...

>   *MARY attempts to straighten CHARLIE's hair.*

CHARLIE   Ah, there's a lady waving at me. Hello! Boy, she's wav-
                    ing really hard. Maybe there's a fire. Something's got her
                    pants in a knot, she's flapping around like an old hen.

MARY   Coming, Mother!

CHARLIE   Your mother? Hello, Mrs. Chalmers! Wonderful tea...!
                    My first tea disaster.

MARY   I should really go and see what she wants before her arm
                    flies off.

CHARLIE   Mm-hm.

MARY   I'll be right back. Don't go anywhere.

CHARLIE   I'll wait right here... flapping around like an old hen?

>   *Rain starts to fall.*

MARY   Then it starts to rain big wet spots on everyone's suits
                    and dresses. And then a downpour. Ladies scream as
                    everyone runs for cover. A dropped teacup shatters. A
                    chair is overturned.

>   *The sky darkens and there is a distant flash of lightning.*
>   *CHARLIE looks straight up and waits.*

                    Charlie should find some shelter, but he just stands there
                    looking up into the sheets of rain. Oh, I told him not to
                    go anywhere.

CHARLIE   One-one thousand, two-one thousand, three-one thou-
                    sand, four-one thous...

Thunder. Mixed into it are an artillery barrage and scattered machine-gun fire.

MARY   That one was closer.

CHARLIE   Mary?

MARY   The storm worsens. Explodes. There are explosions. I see barbed wire.

CHARLIE   This isn't good. This is no good.

MARY   He is knee-deep in mud. He ducks his head into his shoulders as the thunder claps and shells burst. It's his first night at the front.

            Lightning flash.

CHARLIE   One-one thousand, two-one thousand, three-one...

            A thunder clap or a shell crash.

            Oh my God. Oh my God, Mary. Shit.

MARY   I'm right here, Charlie.

CHARLIE   I swear too much.

            Boom.

            Bloody hell! Damn! Damn! Bloody hell! Bullocks!

            Lightning.

MARY   A shell lands close.

            Explosion. Thunder.

            He is showered with mud and rain.

CHARLIE   Oh God, Mary, make it quiet! Make it quiet!

MARY   I can hear him breathing. His heart beating...

CHARLIE   "Cannon in front of them
Volley'd and thunder'd..."

BOTH   "Storm'd at with shot and shell..."

                  Lightning flashes and thunder almost simultaneous.

CHARLIE   We have to get out of here! I have to get out of here!

MARY   Charlie, listen to me! "Boldly they rode and well, into the jaws of Death..." he doesn't listen or he cannot hear or... he was told to stay where he is. That was his last order.

                  CHARLIE panics and begins to abandon his position.

                 Charlie, don't! Just as he is about to run... just as he is about to disobey his orders... another shell comes in, up and behind Charlie, thumps deep into the soaked earth, explodes, and everything throws upwards into the rain.

                  A whistle and a shell burst. CHARLIE is lifted up into the air with the erupting bank. It is suddenly very quiet.

                 Charlie, open your eyes, do you see? Look, just for an instant?

CHARLIE   ...

MARY   For miles the engraved zigzag of the trenches, the water-pocked no man's land reflecting like thousands of perfect mirrors, flights of machine-gun fire streaking quickly bright and out. There again, quickly bright and out. You can see it all from here. Charlie, open your eyes.

CHARLIE crashes back down to the ground.

He sits in the shell hole, chest-deep in water, mud dripping off his nose and helmet. He sits still, trying to sense if all of his body is there with him.

Lightning flashes.

CHARLIE   "Into the mouth of hell
           Rode the six hundred."

Arms. Legs. Fingers. Toes. Ears. I can see. *(laughs)* That was a loud one.

A silence, then a far-off roll of thunder. CHARLIE drags himself up and back onto his feet. He waits under the tree at the tea for MARY.

MARY   Are you all there?

CHARLIE   I think so. Yes. Are you?

MARY   Oh, yes, I'm all here.

A flicker of lightning.

CHARLIE   One-one thousand, two-one thousand, three-one thousand, four-one thousand, five...

Thunder rolls away.

It's going away.

MARY   They always do.

The rain is still lightly falling.

CHARLIE   Is everything all right with your mother?

MARY   Oh, yes. Just a little tea emergency.

CHARLIE   A tea emergency?

MARY   She wanted to know who you were. If you were that
            dirty farm boy with the horse who saw me home the
            other night.

CHARLIE   What did you tell her?

MARY   Does he look like a dirty farm boy?

CHARLIE   What did she say to that?

MARY   I brought an umbrella to rescue you.

                    He takes it just as the rain has faded away.

            I'm sorry I wasn't more of a help to you out here all alone.

CHARLIE   No, I was just about to run off there when I remembered
            your advice. You saved the day.

MARY   "The Charge of the Light Brigade"?

CHARLIE   I'm glad I like it 'cause it's the only one I remember from
            school.

MARY   Why only that one?

CHARLIE   I love the charging on horseback parts, fast with your
            heart all pounding, with your voice just getting ready to
            shout, all on its own. Kind of scary but good, you know?
            Like when I gave you a ride home.

MARY   Oh, it's always like that then.

CHARLIE   Always something like that, only that night there was some-
            thing else that was… different. That I never felt before.

MARY	Me too. What was it, do you think?
CHARLIE	I'm not sure. I think…
MARY	What?
CHARLIE	I think… maybe we could go riding again to…
MARY	I'll be coming back from town tomorrow afternoon. I've got some errands to run for Mother. The post. Perhaps we may bump into each other somewhere along the way?
CHARLIE	Maybe by the old barn?
MARY	By the turn in the road?
CHARLIE	Down from the bridge. Maybe.
MARY	These things do happen sometimes, somewhere along the way.
CHARLIE	They do.
MARY	Oh, Charlie?

He turns back to return her umbrella. She smoothes the bit of hair that was standing up at the back and the umbrella pops open. A steady roll of an artillery barrage can be heard farther off.

"Dear Mary,

"There is not much sitting around allowed in the front line. There are holes and collapses everywhere from the rain and shelling. The water in the trench is a foot deep and the mud is deeper. But we do our best to keep our feet dry…"

How's the letter writing?

CHARLIE   Good. All right. It could be better.

MARY   May I?

> *CHARLIE hands over the letter.*

> "Dear Mary." It starts well. Let's see? "Mud"... "mud"... "mud." Mud, Charlie?

CHARLIE   But I have to tell her something, Sergeant.

FLOWERS   What is it that you'd really like to tell her?

CHARLIE   Things.

FLOWERS   Keeping a brave face for the girl?

> *CHARLIE nods.*

> I should think that she'd like you to write about what's going on in here.

CHARLIE   But how do you write that?

FLOWERS   With your pencil.

> *The artillery barrage intensifies. CHARLIE and FLOWERS look up to where shells whisper over them on their way to the enemy lines.*

> The artillery's up again. Giving them a good pounding.

CHARLIE   You can almost see them. What's it been? Twelve day's worth? Are you going over with the Fifth Battalion's attack?

FLOWERS   I see that you volunteered to go over the top with them?

CHARLIE   They were bound to ask us to go over sooner or later.

FLOWERS	Most of First and Third Troop are going over, that's plenty of volunteers.
CHARLIE	Moss, Givan, and Cook are going.
FLOWERS	In the last week the British haven't gained a mile and there have been more than twelve thousand casualties. One or two more isn't going to make a difference.
CHARLIE	Everyone's got to do their share.
FLOWERS	They need extra stretcher bearers at the dressing station. What about carrying a stretcher?

CHARLIE shakes his head no. FLOWERS nods reluctantly.

All right… don't stop for anything. Keep your spacing. Nice even line. Don't bunch up. Listen for the officer's whistles and we're up.

CHARLIE	You're coming with us?
FLOWERS	Remember, nothing up the pipe, fixed bayonet, that's all. No shooting until we get there.
CHARLIE	Yes, Sergeant.
FLOWERS	Yes, Sergeant. Good.
CHARLIE	Do you think there'll be anyone left alive when we get to them?
FLOWERS	Ah, don't give up hope. Our shelling is probably just keeping them ducking. Listen close for the commands, it's going to be noisy. Charlie?
BOTH	See you on the other side.

The artillery barrage continues its last waves. A watch begins ticking.

CHARLIE   Dear Mary,

               I'm writing this while we wait for the whistles. We're
               part of a big attack tonight. We're packed in like sar-
               dines in the jump-off trench with the Fifth Battalion,
               who are anxious to give the Germans a good go. The
               officers have their eyes on their watches.

MARY   Is that how it was?

CHARLIE   They passed the rum ration around earlier and boy is my
               nose warm.

MARY   Keeping a brave face for the girl?

CHARLIE   Yes.

MARY   Tell me?

CHARLIE   It is hard to breathe. My mouth is dry. No spit. The
               trench is full of men, all of us silent and swallowing.
               Close and damp. Our rifles are held tight and close,
               muzzle up, everyone leaning up against the trench wall.
               Eyes wide, listening, watching the nearest officer. He
               stares at his watch.

MARY   Wiping the mud from the face.

CHARLIE   A minute to two in the morning, the whistle is in his
               mouth.

MARY   His hand shakes.

               The artillery stops and the watch ticking can clearly be heard.

CHARLIE   Then the whistles sound and the first line of the Fifth
               Battalion climb to the top of the trench wall. Right away,
               some of them pitch backwards into us. The German
               machine guns have started their raking. We catch bod-

ies as they fall. Commands come. First line, fix bayonets. At the top they draw their knives and fix them to their rifles. Then the second whistle and the first line march forward out of sight. We all wait and listen to the machine guns.

MARY   It doesn't stop? It continues?

CHARLIE   And then we hear the explosions of the German artillery. More follow. The bullets whistle over our heads and dig into the sand bags and dead bodies at the top.

MARY   What do you do?

CHARLIE   I look up to the stars but there's only sheets of rain lit by the flares. The whistles blow again and the Fifth Battalion's second line clambers to the top of the trench. More of them pitch back onto us. We drag them down. Second line, fix bayonets.

             There is a ring of metal as the bayonets are fixed.

             The whistles blow and the second line begins their march across no man's land. The machine guns continue to rake back and forth but there are rifle shots too. The first line must be shooting. Our boys are firing. Out there, they must have reached the Germans.

MARY   Then it was your turn, like the others?

CHARLIE   Yes. But we didn't walk. Right before we went over, Flowers passed an order down the line. Passed it man to man. Forget about the spacing. Forget about the even lines, you hear me?

MARY   What?

CHARLIE   Run, he said. You understand me? Run as fast as you can.

MARY   Run?

CHARLIE   And I passed it down... run all the way...

MARY   Run all the way... run all the way... run... run all the
              way...

CHARLIE   And we ran as we followed behind the Fifth Battalion.
              We ran through the piles of the killed and wounded
              Fifth Battalion. Strewn out there like old blankets.
              Heaped on top of each other. Beside each other. One
              behind the other. Screaming and grabbing at our legs as
              we ran by them. Over them. Tripping us up.

MARY   And all the while the machine guns kept firing and the
              shells kept falling?

CHARLIE   Yes, Mary. That's the way it was. After the Battle of
              Festubert, our wounded lay in no man's land until night-
              fall when we could go out to get them. Mary, back in our
              trenches, we spent the day listening to them... call to us.

MARY   All those arms and voices.

              *MARY waits by the side of the road. CHARLIE walks up to
              keep their date. He is leading his horse.*

CHARLIE   Hello, Mary.

MARY   Charlie, you made it. I'm so relieved.

CHARLIE   Did you think I wasn't going to?

MARY   I must confess, I was a little worried.

CHARLIE   We practically ran the whole way. You've picked up the
              post.

MARY   And you were just um... passing by...

CHARLIE   Well, since we're both here.... Shall we go for our ride?

MARY   Yes. Yes. Shall we?

CHARLIE   You can get on first.

MARY   Oh.

CHARLIE   Go on, mount up.

MARY   I'm afraid my equitation skills may be a bit rusty.

CHARLIE   We don't mind.

MARY   It's been a while.

CHARLIE   Up you go.

            MARY goes to mount CHARLIE's horse.

            Left side, that's right. Reach up. Both hands like that.
            Just pull and throw your leg over. There you go. Good.

MARY   Are you coming up?

CHARLIE   I'll be up in a minute. You're all right.

            *MARY is mounted up on CHARLIE's horse. She sits very
            straight and still. Silence.*

            You just going to sit there?

MARY   May I walk her a little?

CHARLIE   Well, you look silly just sitting there. Go ahead.

MARY   I've a confession to make. I've never... actually been on a
            horse by myself.

CHARLIE   What? A good English girl like you? Never studied
            equitation?

MARY   Equitation no, ballet and piano yes.

CHARLIE   Ballet, really? Can you dance?

MARY   First position?

CHARLIE   Can you play?

MARY   "God Save the King."

CHARLIE   Well, I guess we'll have to teach you to ride like a
            colonist.

MARY   What do I do first?

CHARLIE   First, we get you up in the saddle.

MARY   We've done that.

CHARLIE   Next we get you moving forward.

MARY   How do we do that?

CHARLIE   You just have to give her the hint.

            *MARY tries to get the horse moving. It stays still. CHARLIE
            looks on. She tries again. Nothing. CHARLIE waits. She thinks
            a moment and does the thing CHARLIE did to get the horse
            going. The horse walks forward.*

MARY   Oh, she just wants to go.

CHARLIE   It just has to be the right hint, that's all.

MARY   Turning right. There we go. Good girl.

CHARLIE   You've got it.

MARY   I've another confession to make.

CHARLIE   You're scared of horses.

MARY smiles.

You didn't seem so afraid when we rode home together?

MARY   Oh I was... but in a different way. I was frightened but you were there, with me, if you know what I mean?

CHARLIE   I think I do. Scary but good.

CHARLIE stops the horse.

MARY   Why are we stopping?

CHARLIE   I don't know.

MARY   I think you do.

He reaches up and touches her face. They kiss. Silence.

Another?

CHARLIE   If it's not too much trouble.

They kiss again.

BOTH   Scary but good.

MARY laughs.

CHARLIE   I like it when you laugh.

MARY   I like laughing at you... I mean, I like it when you make me laugh.

The horse steps forward a little.

Oh!

CHARLIE   Look, we've made her jealous.

MARY laughs and rides the mare around a little.

MARY   Well, she's just going to have to get used to it...

CHARLIE   Look at you. A natural.

MARY   I can't believe I'm doing this.

CHARLIE   Riding a horse?

MARY   Disobeying my mother.

CHARLIE   Is kissing a dirty old farm boy the worst thing you've ever done?

MARY   Best thing I've ever done.

CHARLIE   What would your mother think?

MARY   I'll do much worse.

They kiss again.

What's the worst thing you've ever done? Other than disobeying my mother?

CHARLIE   Other than that? I don't know. I'll tell you when I do it.

What was it? What's that look?

MARY   Nothing.

CHARLIE   I can see it in your eyes. It's not good, is it?

MARY	No. No, I shouldn't have asked. Forget I mentioned it.
CHARLIE	Not now I can't. You have to tell me. Please. Tell me.
MARY	If you really want to know, I'll tell you what it is.
CHARLIE	How do you know?
MARY	You told me in your letter today.
CHARLIE	I really want to know.
MARY	You finally saw a German soldier... please, Charlie, we don't have to talk about this.
CHARLIE	Tell me.
MARY	On patrol, coming back, ten yards from your barbed wire, coming back through no man's land, you looked back before going in to sleep.

Night shades down around them.

CHARLIE	Do you see that? Right there, see?

Silence while they watch.

Right-there-right-there, Sergeant.

FLOWERS	...
CHARLIE	Do you see him?
FLOWERS	Who is it?
CHARLIE	A scout or... or a sniper?
FLOWERS	One of ours?

CHARLIE   No... I don't know. I don't know. No.

FLOWERS   ...

CHARLIE   What should we do?

FLOWERS   We drop him. If he crosses that line, take him.

CHARLIE   I see.

FLOWERS   ...

CHARLIE   Go back. Come on, go back...

Go back, go back, please go back...

> *CHARLIE continues this mantra through MARY's next speech.*

MARY   The sniper, the ghost, the German... person came closer, from puddle to puddle and you wished he'd go back, you wished he would but he kept disappearing and appearing, closer, like he was trying to catch up, to your patrol... until he crossed the line. You held your breath. Then Flowers touched your shoulder and your rifle made the sound...

> *CHARLIE's mantra stops.*

Of one quick stroke of an axe chopping wood.

> *Crack. Silence.*

CHARLIE   There was a splash too, a splash, when he dropped into the water.

MARY   Through your sights you saw this, while the spent casing was still hot in the smoking barrel, still pointed where he'd been standing. He bobbed up like he was looking up in a lake in the summer, with the water ringing out around him. But then, slowly, he floated over onto his front.

CHARLIE   It's the worst thing I ever did.

> *Quiet. MARY comes over and puts her arms around CHARLIE. They hold onto each other very gently and innocently.*

MARY   Oh, look, Charlie, how pretty a night it is. The stars are coming out. Look there...

CHARLIE   It is pretty. God, I miss this.

MARY   Charlie?

CHARLIE   Hmm?

MARY   There is something I'd like to say to you.

CHARLIE   Me too.

MARY   Charlie, I... I...

CHARLIE   You what?

MARY   We've got lots of time.

CHARLIE   That's what you wanted to say to me?

MARY   Something like that, yes.

> *They both close their eyes. She caresses his hair. He is very still. MARY listens for a moment and then whispers.*

Charlie? It's time to wake up, sleepy head.

> *He is still silent.*

MARY   Wake up, Charlie, wake up.

CHARLIE   Are we going over again, Sergeant?

FLOWERS   No, trooper, we're not going over. How are you doing?

CHARLIE   Fine.

FLOWERS   How are your feet? All right? Keeping them dry?

CHARLIE   Ya.

FLOWERS   At least one of us is. Were you dreaming?

CHARLIE   Ya, about the German that we shot on patrol.

FLOWERS   Don't think so much. Don't let yourself think so much.

CHARLIE   I wasn't thinking. That's the trouble. I was dreaming.

FLOWERS   Well, dream about this then. I've got news. We're
                relieved. So pack up, fifteen minutes.

CHARLIE   Are we getting our horses back?

FLOWERS   It's not that news. We get to go out, rest, clean up for a
                couple of weeks, then we're back in the line.

CHARLIE   Where?

FLOWERS   Here. Or somewhere else. I don't know.

CHARLIE   In the line though?

FLOWERS   In the line. Where else?

                CHARLIE walks away. MARY turns from him.

CHARLIE   Dear Mary,

We all look forward to getting out of the line. We do our best to get the lice out of our clothes and get a little sleep. This time out we are camped by an abandoned barn. Halfway through the night, I go inside, to get out of the rain. It doesn't help because of the shell holes in the roof. But it's still nicer inside because it feels like our barn.

> *CHARLIE closes his eyes.*

I look for you there. It's so easy.

> *The sky gleams through the slats and roof holes of the barn. MARY sits and reads.*

MARY
"Down she came and found a boat
Beneath a willow left afloat,
And round about the prow she wrote
'The Lady of Shalott.'"

CHARLIE
Mary.

MARY
Charlie, there you are.

CHARLIE
You're all alone.

MARY
Just me and a little poetry. "The Lady of Shalott."

CHARLIE
What's it about?

MARY
A maiden who falls in love with a knight.

CHARLIE
Sounds nice.

MARY
He can't love her so she dies of heartbreak floating down the river.

CHARLIE
Ow. Really? That's sad. Does she drown or go over the falls or something?

MARY   No, she dies of heartbreak for him.

CHARLIE   She doesn't fall in the river?

MARY   Her unfulfilled love for him is enough to make her die
            of heartbreak. That's the way it's done. Listen.

            "For ere she reached upon the tide
            The first house by the water-side,
            Singing in her song she died,
            The Lady of Shalott."

CHARLIE   I see.

MARY   How did you know I was here?

CHARLIE   Where else would I find you?

MARY   Did you go by my house?

CHARLIE   I rode past. Said hello to your mother.

MARY   You didn't?

CHARLIE   I rode up and asked if you were around.

MARY   What did she say?

CHARLIE   She said you were out with a boy...

MARY   My mother said that? Wonderful!

CHARLIE   Oh, she was nice.

MARY   She didn't say anything else to you?

CHARLIE   No, nothing else.

MARY   Nothing at all? She was on her best behaviour then. She's got her mind set on the kind of gentlemen that I should marry.

CHARLIE   Not one of the colonists?

MARY   Not dirty farm-boy colonists anyway. Well, Charlie, you've found me out, I'm secretly in love with Alfred Lord Tennyson. It's been quite torrid out here in the barn.

CHARLIE   I was thinking, Mary... that maybe I'm... not... the right sort of...

MARY   On the train trip here I saw them every so often... old sway-backed barns with an empty windowed farmhouse. I wonder who lived here? I wonder where the people have gone? Do you know what I mean?

CHARLIE   Somewhere new?

MARY   Somewhere happier where they can start over?

CHARLIE   Maybe they got a better quarter section a day east of here.

MARY   Poo. That's not very poetic. Perhaps this place has got bad memories hiding in it somewhere. Something not to be remembered. Like ghosts?

CHARLIE   Like ghosts. Now, it's just us here.

MARY   Only we're not ghosts.

            Stay with me.

CHARLIE   I have to go.

MARY   Charlie, wait.

But Charlie doesn't wait. He leaves because of my mother. He leaves because he loves me. I don't know why he leaves. I see him working on his father's farm. I see him from the road when I pass. He works very hard. He doesn't look up. He thinks work will help him forget. But he's wrong.

CHARLIE works at the sandbags again.

Stop a minute and listen to me.

CHARLIE   These sandbags need a little work here, Sergeant.

FLOWERS   I was talking to the quartermaster... Charlie!

CHARLIE keeps working.

Put the bag down, Trooper!

CHARLIE   Sergeant.

FLOWERS   I want to talk to you.

CHARLIE   I was listening.

FLOWERS   I know. Just sit down for a minute. How are you doing? Cold not getting to you? Hey, Charlie, keeping warm?

CHARLIE   I'm fine.

FLOWERS   Listen, I was looking at the records and it looks like you've been out in no man's land every night this week? And I hear you've volunteered to go out on patrol again tonight?

CHARLIE   Everyone's got to do their share.

FLOWERS   Yes, their share, not everyone else's. You'll tire yourself out. You'll get knocked on some stupid patrol around in the mud—or even worse you'll get me knocked. Is there something you want to tell me?

CHARLIE   No.

FLOWERS   Nothing at all?

CHARLIE   No. Nothing.

FLOWERS   You're not going out tonight. No patrols for you until I say so.

CHARLIE   But, Sergeant…

FLOWERS   Save yourself. You don't want to use yourself up before your big charge… before you get back to Mary, do you? All right then, it's settled, you're staying in tonight. It's settled, right? Yes, Sergeant, is the answer to that question.

CHARLIE   Yes, Sergeant.

> *Night falls and with it big, glowing snowflakes.*

MARY   I see the nights and patrols pass in no man's land and Charlie sits out. I see the nightly ambushes. I see the surprised grenades tossed over at each other. I see them drag back the dead. Flowers keeps him out of for as long as he can but the night comes when Charlie must take his turn.

> *MARY stands above him as CHARLIE crawls by on patrol.*

He crawls by in the snow. He is nearly by me and he looks up and I see him.

CHARLIE   An angel. There are angels on the moon.

MARY   He just looks at me and I look at him. Then there is shooting. They fire into the dark and somewhere out in the dark there are voices and arms that fire back.

> *A sudden burst of rifle fire. CHARLIE is hit. The volley con-*
> *tinues and sporadically lessens to occasional popping.*

Charlie's blood melts the snow under him. The men of
the patrol crowd in, drag him up and huddle him back
to their line. I can only watch as they drag him further
and further away through the snow. And as they do he
looks back down a long red streak to see if I am still
standing here, waiting.

Soon, I am the only one left out here in a place that looks
like the moon. I am alone on the moon and Charlie is
bleeding somewhere far away. I can do nothing about it.
I never can do anything about it. And just like it always
does, war begins and I cannot do anything about it.

> *CHARLIE approaches MARY.*

CHARLIE   Mary, have you heard?

MARY   Yes, I've heard. It's all my mother and father have been
               talking about. It's all anyone can talk about.

CHARLIE   "By midnight tonight if the kaiser doesn't withdraw his
               troops from Belgian soil, Great Britain will be at war
               with Germany."

MARY   Do you think he'll withdraw?

CHARLIE   Germany says they only invaded because they think the
               French plan to attack them through Belgium. They say
               they're only protecting themselves.

MARY   If they're only protecting themselves, why is everyone
               attacking each other?

CHARLIE   Well, they've all pledged to protect each other.

MARY   Is this why you came to talk to me? I haven't seen you in
            weeks and now you're here to tell me we might be going
            to war?

CHARLIE   I've been working for my father.

MARY   Why haven't you come around? It's because of my
            mother, isn't it?

CHARLIE   I thought that, maybe... you might be able to... you
            know... wake up and find someone a bit better suited for
            you.

MARY   A bit better suited for me? Like who?

CHARLIE   Someone who... someone who is...

MARY   What? Richer? Smarter?

CHARLIE   No.

MARY   Then who? I don't care what my mother thinks.

            CHARLIE turns away.

            What's the matter? Nothing has changed, do you think
            something has changed? Why?

CHARLIE   I didn't want it to.

MARY   Then why haven't I heard from you?

CHARLIE   What do I have to say?

MARY   What do you have to say.

            She takes a letter from CHARLIE's hand.

            Let's see, what do you have to say?

She opens it and reads.

"Dear Mary,

"I have been wounded." Oh, my God. Where?

He looks with surprise to his wound.

CHARLIE   In the east of France.

MARY   Charlie!

CHARLIE   Here.

He shows her the wound.

MARY   Oh, my poor Charlie!

CHARLIE   It'll be all right in the end, Mary. We will be happy.

MARY   Of course we will.

CHARLIE   Everything will be all right in the end.

MARY   Of course, everything will be all right, Charlie.

She pulls his shirt aside to see the spot where the bullet entered. She gently touches it with the tip of her finger.

CHARLIE   Ow.

FLOWERS   Trooper, steady up, man!

CHARLIE's wound has healed. They both look at its progress.

Ah, is that what the big fuss was about? You might be able to impress your girl with that.... What, did they use two whole inches of thread on that?

CHARLIE	They did a pretty good job, Sergeant.
FLOWERS	Wrong rank. You owe me a beer for that one.
CHARLIE	Oh, my God, you've been promoted. No more working for a living?
FLOWERS	That's right, Trooper, it's Lieutenant Flowers from now on.
CHARLIE	An officer?
FLOWERS	Who'd have thought?
CHARLIE	Did they give you First Troop?
FLOWERS	No.
CHARLIE	Aw, Second?
FLOWERS	No.
CHARLIE	What? Don't tell me supply?
FLOWERS	The Squadron.
CHARLIE	C Squadron Commander! That's wonderful.
FLOWERS	Scary but good.
CHARLIE	When did this happen?
FLOWERS	You've been out for a while now. They didn't just end the war because Charlie couldn't be in it.
CHARLIE	Well, then…
FLOWERS	Shall we get it over with?

CHARLIE   Congratulations, sir!

                 They salute and shake hands.

FLOWERS   Well, I guess you're ready to come back to us unless you
                 got a hangnail you want them to look at.

CHARLIE   They said I could go yesterday.

FLOWERS   Then I've got a surprise for you.

                 CHARLIE stops in his tracks. He's seen their horses.

CHARLIE   We've got our horses back.

FLOWERS   No more infantry duty for us. We're in reserve, waiting
                 for a breakthrough. But it's been pretty quiet up front.

CHARLIE   Really? I still hear some shelling.

FLOWERS   Ah, the Germans, they just drop three or four every now
                 and then, in case they might get lucky. I think it means
                 the fight is out of them, we've got them on the run. Here,
                 I picked this one out for you.

CHARLIE   Hello there.

                 CHARLIE inspects his horse.

FLOWERS   They're as healthy as you are. Healthier maybe. They've
                 had more exercise.

CHARLIE   It's all the hospital food.

                 CHARLIE touches and pats her.

                 We going to save the day me and you? Sure, we can. Sure,
                 we will.

FLOWERS   Are you two going to stand around necking all day? Or are we going to see if you still know how to ride after all this time crawling around in the mud?

CHARLIE   That sounds like a challenge to me.

> *CHARLIE mounts up.*

FLOWERS   Take it however you like.

> *CHARLIE and FLOWERS line themselves up on their horses and when they are ready they begin the race.*

CHARLIE   Say when?

MARY   When!

We race out of the hospital yard and out into the sunny countryside. We fly past the slow ambulance trucks on the dirt roads. The hedgerows and fields and trees shade us for flickering moments and we flash again into the afternoon brightness. The trees come up fast and through their leaves the sky flashes by like water on a pond. He gets smaller as I watch him from higher and higher.

I am his air and wind. I am his swirling sky looking down above him. Up here it's quiet when I am still, and when I listen closely I can hear his horse's hooves and the sound of his laughing voice.

CHARLIE   Hold on, we'll be home soon!

MARY   And as he disappears and the sun begins to set I can smell rain coming.

> *MARY takes in the smell of the rain. CHARLIE approaches very gently. He stops and lets her breathe a few more times before interrupting. The sky flickers with far-off lightning.*

CHARLIE   Did you hear the news?

MARY   Yes, Charlie. Yes, I did. Who hasn't?

CHARLIE   "Germany declared war on Great Britain..."

MARY   "...and Canada pledged her support by offering troops."
              That's what the headlines say. What did they really
              expect to happen? How did you get past my mother?

CHARLIE   She let me in, said you were reading in here.

MARY   She invited you in? She's changed her opinion of farm
              boys and colonists all of a sudden.

CHARLIE   I think maybe she liked me after all.

MARY   I think she likes you more now that you're going to fight
              for the British Empire.

CHARLIE   How do you know I'm going?

MARY   Isn't everybody? That's all they're talking about in town.
              All the men in my father's office are signing up together.

CHARLIE   Everyone must do their share.

MARY   Charlie.

CHARLIE   I went to militia camp last summer with my cousin.

MARY   So?

CHARLIE   I can shoot.

MARY   So what? That's what they're all saying at my father's
              office, but they're all just clerks. They file papers and fill
              their pens and now they think they're soldiers?

CHARLIE   I can ride.

MARY   I know you can. But you don't have to.

CHARLIE   I want to join the cavalry. I've always wanted to. Like in "The Charge of the Light Brigade."

MARY   Like in "The Charge of the Light Brigade"? Do you listen to yourself when you speak it? "Not tho' the soldier knew someone had blunder'd? Into the jaws of Death? Into the mouth of hell?"

CHARLIE   "But when can their glory fade? Honour the charge they made!"

MARY   That's poetry, Charlie, not real life.

CHARLIE   They need men who can ride. I can ride. I love to ride. You know what it's like, Mary. The wind and the sky? Your heart beating faster, louder than the hooves. You remember?

MARY   I just thought...

CHARLIE   What? Tell me.

MARY   I thought that it was us. I thought it was us, the wind and the sky, faster and louder than the hooves. If you don't come home I'll die of heartbreak.

CHARLIE   That's poetry, Mary, not real life.

            She turns away. Silence.

            I have to go.

MARY   Then go.

CHARLIE   I want to ask you... if you'll meet me in the barn tonight.

MARY	For what? *(pause)* Why?
CHARLIE	There's something I want ask you.
MARY	No, I won't. Not if you're going to go.
CHARLIE	But Mary…
MARY	If you are going to war then go. I don't care. I won't stop you.
CHARLIE	Please, meet me in the barn.
MARY	I said go away! *(pause)* GO!

CHARLIE walks away.

I see Charlie after he left my house. He walks his horse down the road through the puddles left by the dark rain heading far away east. I always wish right then for him to come back. For him to turn around and come back to me, and he almost does. He almost turns back, but then he remembers I told him to go and he slowly follows after the flickering lightning at the edge of the sky.

The sky flickers with lightning far off.

CHARLIE	Sir? What's the news?
FLOWERS	Charlie, I was daydreaming for a second there.

FLOWERS looks off at the horizon.

CHARLIE	Are we moving out?
FLOWERS	Yes, Charlie. Ten minutes. Maybe.
CHARLIE	Do you know what's up?

FLOWERS	The enemy has been saving it up for one last offensive. They hit the French hard and punched a hundred-mile hole in the line.
CHARLIE	A hundred-mile hole in the line?
FLOWERS	They're just holding now until they bring up their reinforcements, then they're going to gather steam in a straight line headed for Paris.
CHARLIE	Our brigade's got the job to fill in the hole?
FLOWERS	We of the Canadian cavalry are to hold as long as we can until the infantry can re-form defences behind us.
CHARLIE	If we don't?
FLOWERS	Then they're going to roll right into Paris. And that'll be it. From the sounds of it, there's a lot of them.
CHARLIE	Across the river there?
FLOWERS	They're thick in the woods there, Moreuil Wood it's called. It's us, and the rest of the division. We're going to attack it.
CHARLIE	For sure?
FLOWERS	Sounds like it. As sure as it ever gets.
CHARLIE	Mounted? Maybe we'll take them in a charge, just like we said?
FLOWERS	Maybe, Charlie. But orders are to ride up and fight our way through the woods on foot.
CHARLIE	It's better than the trenches.
FLOWERS	It is that. How's everyone?

CHARLIE   Standing to.

FLOWERS   Charlie?

CHARLIE   Yes, sir.

                What is it?

                        FLOWERS smiles.

FLOWERS   Nothing. You ready? Mount up.

CHARLIE   We're going to charge, Mary. I'm going to get to charge.
                We cross the bridge. Our biplanes take passes at the
                Wood, dropping bombs down into the branches. By the
                time we're over, the other cavalry squadrons are already
                fighting dismounted in the Wood.

MARY   Like hundreds of champagne corks popping.

CHARLIE   We ride forward to dismount and join in, when the gen-
                eral rides up and Flowers halts us.

MARY   A change of plans?

CHARLIE   Flowers turns to us. Listen up, boys. We don't attack
                here with the others. The general thinks we can work
                in through the back of the Wood and meet up with our
                boys in the middle. Surround them. We're going for a
                ride.

MARY   That's good news. It's going well.

CHARLIE   We just have to go for a ride. With any luck we'll catch
                them retreating. We're all excited and the horses can smell
                it. We head off. It's like riding in the fields back home.
                Pretty and easy, the bounce in the saddle, the spring in
                my legs. The sound of our harness, like sleigh bells.

We round the back of Moreuil Wood, out in the open. Fields of blue and green, waves like the ocean. And men in the waves. Flowers stands up tall in the saddle to see. Enemy troops set in two lines, fixed bayonets, a cannon. Machine guns on the flanks. An ambush.

MARY   Oh, God, they're waiting for you.

CHARLIE   They open fire. There are hits among us. My mare's ears flick. The cannon fires and dirt spits up, a horse screams, things fly through the air. We can't turn back. Flowers rings out his sabre.

MARY   It's a charge, Charlie, it's a charge!

CHARLIE   We flash all our sabres bare and our horses race to catch up with him. The long blades of grass blend together and blur with speed. I crouch low with my head beside hers. She breathes.

MARY   Shh ha, shh ha, shh ha.

CHARLIE   Flowers is flying, his sabre rolling over and over in forward circles, waving the charge on. He is shouting. I can hear it through my stirrups into my spurs and boots. I am catching up to you, Flowerdew!

BOTH   CHARGE! CHARGE! CHARGE!

CHARLIE is giddy with excitement.

CHARLIE   His foot loses a stirrup. His horse twists and tumbles. Flowers is down. We leap over them. We are charging, Mary. I am charging faster than anyone ever.

MARY stands with her eyes closed.

MARY   One-one thousand, two-one thousand, thr...

CHARLIE   Before I plunge into the smoke, a bird flashes across our path. His wings flicker three times and he pushes himself, flicker three times, and we're gone by him. My sabre pulls my shoulder as it pierces a man there. Right through the line we break and we charge the kneeling second line.

MARY   One-one thousand, two-one...

CHARLIE   One of them raises his rifle to shield himself. I club at his head. My sabre falls in once, twice, three times. She leaps forward again, panicked, for the open fields. She wants to keep running until her heart bursts. I pull hard on her, to bring her around to attack again and then... I see what's behind me.

Beyond the man I'd just cut down there was the confusion we'd crashed into, like an ocean wave. Germans and Canadians, some still shooting, some crawling behind the cover of dead horses. A trooper, I don't know who, carrying another like a three-legged race. Then they both fall. Another trying to remount his horse with one arm dripping red beside him. His foot kept slipping. And amongst all that, one horse was grazing, calmly picking at the grass as if he'd spent his whole life chewing in an old farmer's field.

MARY   RUN, CHARLIE, RUN! PLEASE!

CHARLIE   And then I wake, kick her to a run and we race for the Wood. I dismount and fire at the cannon, at the lines of Germans, at the machine guns on their flanks. When they're dead I fire at the men retreating. I fire. I reload. I fire. I reload. I fire. I reload. I fire. I sight a man careful. I fire. I do not get tired of it.

        The sound of battle fades. Then single shots rise with pauses in between. CHARLIE sits and breathes in near exhaustion.

MARY quietly approaches.

MARY	Charlie, are you all right?
CHARLIE	I twisted my shoulder a little.
MARY	Not a scratch. I saw you.
CHARLIE	You did?
MARY	You did it. You got your charge.
CHARLIE	Hold still, Flowers, the stretcher bearers will be here in a minute.

FLOWERS staggers from his wounds. CHARLIE catches him and eases him to the ground.

FLOWERS	You're all right?
CHARLIE	My mare's got a nicked hoof... sir, hold still, don't move.
FLOWERS	Couple of good ones through the legs.
CHARLIE	They're not that bad.
FLOWERS	Bad enough I think... 'twil serve.
CHARLIE	No sir, no sir. You won a ticket home.
FLOWERS	I'll be making the crossing without you.
CHARLIE	You'll... you'll be up in no time.
FLOWERS	Is there anyone else?
CHARLIE	There are a lot left. They're coming in, lots wounded. Looks like you'll have lots of company in the hospital.

FLOWERS   What's all that shooting?

CHARLIE   That's... that's the horses, sir.

FLOWERS   Are there a lot of them hurt?

CHARLIE   Yes, sir, there are a lot of them hurt, they're putting them
                 down. We're back to the mud. I heard someone firing
                 their pistol after you went down. Was that you?

FLOWERS   Took a few shots at that cannon.

CHARLIE   Someone said they're putting you up for a VC.

                 FLOWERS doesn't hear. He is fading quickly.

FLOWERS   ...Charlie?

CHARLIE   Ya.

FLOWERS   I saw you. From where we fell. I was pinned under but
                 I could still see. You were there first. You charged. You
                 got to charge.

CHARLIE   I thought everyone was right behind me.

FLOWERS   You went through both lines.

CHARLIE   I didn't know I was the only one. I thought everyone
                 was right behind me but I was really just by myself. The
                 charge, it wasn't... poetry.

FLOWERS   Charlie, listen to me, are there two lines of Germans
                 there now?

CHARLIE   No. Not anymore.

FLOWERS   Then we did our share. That will have to be enough. I told you, you'd see her everywhere you looked.

CHARLIE   She's in everything.

FLOWERS fades and CHARLIE turns away.

Dearest Mary,

There is no more Flowers.

I want to meet you in our barn. I never want to leave you again. I miss you more than anything. I miss you so much. I want to be home with you and never leave you again. I will love you and you will be happy. I promise you that. In the end you will be happy.

Love...

CHARLIE waits for MARY in the barn.

MARY   And this is how it ends. I never went to see him, but in this dream I do. We're in the barn. Charlie is. He is waiting for me. Nervous and shy, waiting to sail away on the grey ship full of horses.

The night that I never came to say goodbye. It's the night he waited to ask me and he left the next morning. But in this dream I go to see him. I go to stop him. I go to tell him.

CHARLIE   Mary?

I'm glad you came.

MARY   You didn't think I would, did you?

CHARLIE   I wasn't too sure.

MARY   So, you're going?

CHARLIE   I am. I am. I have to. It'll be over soon. We'll take them
               in a charge outside of a year. That's what they're all say-
               ing. We'll be home by Christmas. It won't seem that long
               and I'll be home.

               CHARLIE is less convinced of this than he was.

               I'll write you non-stop, you'll see. Your mailbox will be
               full all the time. I promise. You won't even miss me.

MARY   Yes, I will. Yes, I do. I miss you very badly. Every minute.

CHARLIE   It'll be over before you...

MARY   Charlie...

CHARLIE   Then we can be married.

MARY   Yes, that would be wonderful.

CHARLIE   It'll be sunny. You'll be in one of those pretty white
               dresses and we can have our portrait taken and we can
               have children. We'll have children, not right away. Two
               girls and one boy...

MARY   Two boys and one girl.

CHARLIE   ...and we'll have horses for all the little colonists.

MARY   Charlie, listen, for a minute, please. It sounds lovely
               but... just listen. I went to get the post today.

CHARLIE   Did I write?

MARY   There wasn't anything there.

CHARLIE	Oh. Well, I bet there will be something tomorrow. Or the day after. You know how slow the mail is.
MARY	There won't be any more letters.
CHARLIE	Sure, there will. I write you all the time. I just promised.
MARY	The last one that arrived was the one after the charge at Moreuil Wood. The one where you told me you wanted to come home. You said, "I want to come home now. I want to meet you in our barn. I never want to leave you again."

Something is slowly dawning on CHARLIE.

CHARLIE	What is it, Mary? What happened?
MARY	I met your father today in town.
CHARLIE	How's he doing? I miss him already.
MARY	He misses you too. The farm is well. There are two new mares. He said that he'd... that he'd gotten a message. News.
CHARLIE	Did Flowers get his medal?
MARY	Yes.
CHARLIE	Lieutenant Gordon Muriel Flowerdew, Victoria Cross.
MARY	It's hard to forget a name like that. No, it was a telegram. You and the Canadian Cavalry Division stopped the German advance. Some say you saved the war.
CHARLIE	That's good, isn't it?
MARY	It is good, I suppose. I'm trying. I'm trying. You were in a field. You and all of your tents. A German plane

flew by at night and strafed the regiment while you were camped.

CHARLIE   Was anyone hurt?

             She shakes her head.

MARY   (*whispers*) No.

CHARLIE   How about the horses?

MARY   No, but they were scattered... and you had to, all of you had to go and find them where they'd run off to. And it took all night to find the horses and... the German artillery was shelling places where there might be regiments camped out. They just dropped three or four every now and then, in case they might get... in case they might happen to drop some shells on some- one who might happen to be out there. Out there look- ing for their horses.

CHARLIE   They do that all the time. It's a sign that we've got them on the run, that they're getting desperate. The fight is out of them.

MARY   But Charlie, I have to tell you... I have to tell you. You've come and found her in a field. She wakes up from her dream and stands up. You touch her and step by her neck and shoulder. You calm her. The sun is rising. You're happy. She's happy. She is unhurt and you can bring her back home. I dream it all the time.

CHARLIE   That's when they shelled the field?

MARY   I swear you hear them. You look up at the sky. The two of you don't move and I always wonder why. You just stand beside her looking up at the sky.

CHARLIE   We're going to count the thousands from the flash to the rumble.

MARY   Yes.

CHARLIE   Before they land... before I... before I die... do I say anything?

MARY   Yes. Something. I can't make it out. I'm sorry.

CHARLIE   I guess we won't be getting married. I guess we don't.

MARY   I'm sorry.

CHARLIE   I'm sorry, too.

MARY holds CHARLIE's face in her hands.

MARY   I nearly die of heartache. I swear, for months I can't move. For months I float down the river with my name on the prow.

CHARLIE   But you get better though.

MARY   I do.

CHARLIE   You don't die.

MARY   I live.

CHARLIE   You love someone good. Please tell me you marry someone good?

MARY   Not yet. Tomorrow.

CHARLIE   Just love him as well as you can and be happy. Please.

MARY   I'm sorry, Charlie, I'm sorry I never came to see you in the barn.

CHARLIE   You did tonight.

MARY   I'm sorry I never stopped you from going.

CHARLIE   You did tonight.

MARY   I'm so sorry. It's the worst thing I ever did. And I can't forget you.

CHARLIE   Don't forget. Just let go.

MARY   I'm trying to. It's just you're in everything. All the time.

CHARLIE   Let me be in everything. Just a little less maybe.

MARY   Will you always be there?

CHARLIE   Yes, Mary, always. Only a little less. I've got to go now.

               A far-off roll of thunder sounds. MARY and CHARLIE look to it.

MARY   No, don't go. Don't go. Please, stay with me.

CHARLIE   I can't stay. I have to go now and it's time for you to wake up.

MARY   I can't.

CHARLIE   Yes, you can.

MARY   Please, don't go. Kiss me, please.

               They kiss. They hold on very tight.

CHARLIE   I love you.

MARY   I love you so much.

CHARLIE   You... you are the best thing, the very best thing. I'll see you someday.

MARY   I hope so. I do hope so.

CHARLIE slowly lets go of MARY.

There's a thunderstorm coming.

CHARLIE   I don't mind getting a little wet.

MARY   What are you going to do?

CHARLIE   I don't know. I think... I think I'll just go and... I think I'll just go for a ride... I'll just go out for a little ride in the fields. Just enjoy the rain for a little while.

MARY's composure begins to slip.

Don't worry, it'll be over by the time you wake up. Mary's wedding will be sunny. You'll never dream this again. In a little while you are going to wake up and I will have been lying under the grass for nearly two years now. You are going to wake up and you will never have this dream again. And when you wake up this is what I see:

I see you in a white dress at the church. I see your mother and friends helping you with your hair and yellow flowers. And you are beautiful. I can see tears on your face as you walk down the aisle with all your friends and family smiling for you. People think you are crying because of all the excitement. You walk slowly with your face looking at the floor. You try very hard to take every step. And just before you get up to the front, your eyes slowly rise and you see the face of the good man you are going to marry. And slowly, like a sunrise, you smile and your heart is like the clear blue sky. You smile, Mary.

And outside a soft wind blows, and in that wind there is the very faint sound of a horse riding in the fields.

Just barely it's there, faint in the summer wind.

MARY   How do you know?

CHARLIE   Because I'm in it.

> *The sound of a light breeze can be heard. CHARLIE stands off in the deep blue, but is not gone.*

MARY   And that's the end of the dream. It begins at the end and ends at the beginning. Like before, Charlie rides away thinking of me, only this time he doesn't go away. This time there is no more war. This time he rides off into the fields.

When I awake, the day, my dress, and my husband are waiting. It's a July wedding on a Saturday morning in nineteen hundred and twenty. I still think of him.

I see him on horses. I see him running with them, in dreams, in waking, in forests, in evenings and in mornings. I hear him laughing and riding swiftly through fields. I hear him in church bells. I see white dresses, flowers, and little babies and Charlie is there in all of it. Only, now a little less. Only, now a little bit less. And that will be enough. Goodbye, Charlie.

CHARLIE   Goodbye, Mary. Do you want to know what I say before the shells land?

MARY   Yes, please.

CHARLIE   Wake up, Mary, wake up.

They smile at each other from a distance. Then, as they leave separately, the wind rises a little and the church bells ring. Behind that, farther off as the sun rises, a single horse rides away into the distance.

All of this is very pretty.

End.

Acknowledgements

I wish to extend my thanks to all of the theatres and agencies involved in the writing and development of *Mary's Wedding*: the Alberta Foundation for the Arts, the Alberta Playwrights' Network, Workshop West's Springboards New Play Festival, and the 2000 Banff Playwrights Colony—a partnership between the Canada Council for the Arts and Alberta Theatre Projects. I would like to cite the book *Stand to Your Horses* by Captain S.H. Williams MC as an important source and influence on the play. "The Charge Of the Light Brigade" and "The Lady of Shallott" were written by Alfred Lord Tennyson. Thank you too to the Museum of the Regiments and the men of the Lord Strathcona's Horse (Royal Canadians) Regimental Museum and Archives for allowing me to include Flowerdew's letter and photo in this publication. Also, thanks gentlemen, for the loan of the boots and spurs for opening night. My sincere admiration and appreciation goes to the actors and directors who have lent themselves to Mary and Charlie throughout the development of the play. They are: Ravonna Dow, Ryan Luhning, Heather Inglis, Medina Hahn, Daniel Arnold, Ron Jenkins, Aviva Amour-Ostroff, Greg Spottiswood, Jenny Young, Saxon Decocq, Tracey Ferencz, and Ian Leung. Thank you to Michael Healey, John Murrell, Sharon Pollock, Ian Prinsloo, Linda Gaboriau, Bob White, Micheline Chevrier, Marti Maraden, and Roy Surette for their encouragement. A special thanks, however, must go to two of the play's most devout: Vanessa Porteous and Gina Wilkinson for their loving work and support.

—SM

Stephen's award-winning plays *Looking After Eden*, *Pervert*, and *The Boy's Own Jedi Handbook* series originated at Calgary's Ground Zero Theatre. In 2002, his play *Mary's Wedding* premiered at Alberta Theatre Projects' playRites Festival and won the 2000 Alberta Playwriting Competition, the 2002 Betty Mitchell Award for Best New Play, and the 2003 Alberta Literary Award for Drama. *Mary's Wedding* continues to be produced throughout the US, Canada, and the UK. In 2006, *The Oxford Roof Climber's Rebellion* was produced as a co-production between the Tarragon Theatre and the Great Canadian Theatre Company, and was a hit off-Broadway in 2007. The play won the 2007 Canadian Author's Association Carol Bolt Award for the best English-language play and the 2007 Gwen Paris Ringwood Award of the Alberta Literary Awards for best play. Stephen's filmwriting credits include *Ginger Snaps Back: The Beginning* and *The Dark*. He has a BFA in Drama from the University of Calgary. For more info, go to www.stephenmassicotte.com.